THE NATURE KIDS GUIDE TO
LEOPARDS

DAVID ANDERSON

LP Media Inc. Publishing

For information address LP Media Inc. Publishing,
30012 Variolite St NW, Princeton MN 55371
www.lpmedia.org

Publication Data

Leopards
The Nature Kid's Guide to Leopards — First edition.

Summary: "Learn all about Leopards, the Nature Kid Way"
— Provided by publisher.

ISBN: 979-8-89818-108-6

[1. Leopards - Non-Fiction] I. Title.

Title: The Nature Kid's Guide to Leopards

CONTENTS

WILD WORLDS

DID YOU KNOW?
Leopards are the strongest climbers of all big cats. They can carry prey twice their own weight up into trees to keep it safe from other animals.

Growl! A leopard crouches in tall grass. Its golden eyes scan the land.

Leopards live in many different **habitats**. Some make their homes in hot, dry grasslands. Others live in thick rainforests with tall trees.

These big cats can survive in cold places too. Snow Leopards live high on snowy mountains where the air is thin and icy.

Leopards also live near fresh water. You can find them by rivers and in wet swamps. Some even survive in dry deserts with little rain.

Their spotted coats help them blend in anywhere. Rain or shine, these cats find a way to thrive.

SPOTTED SPOTS

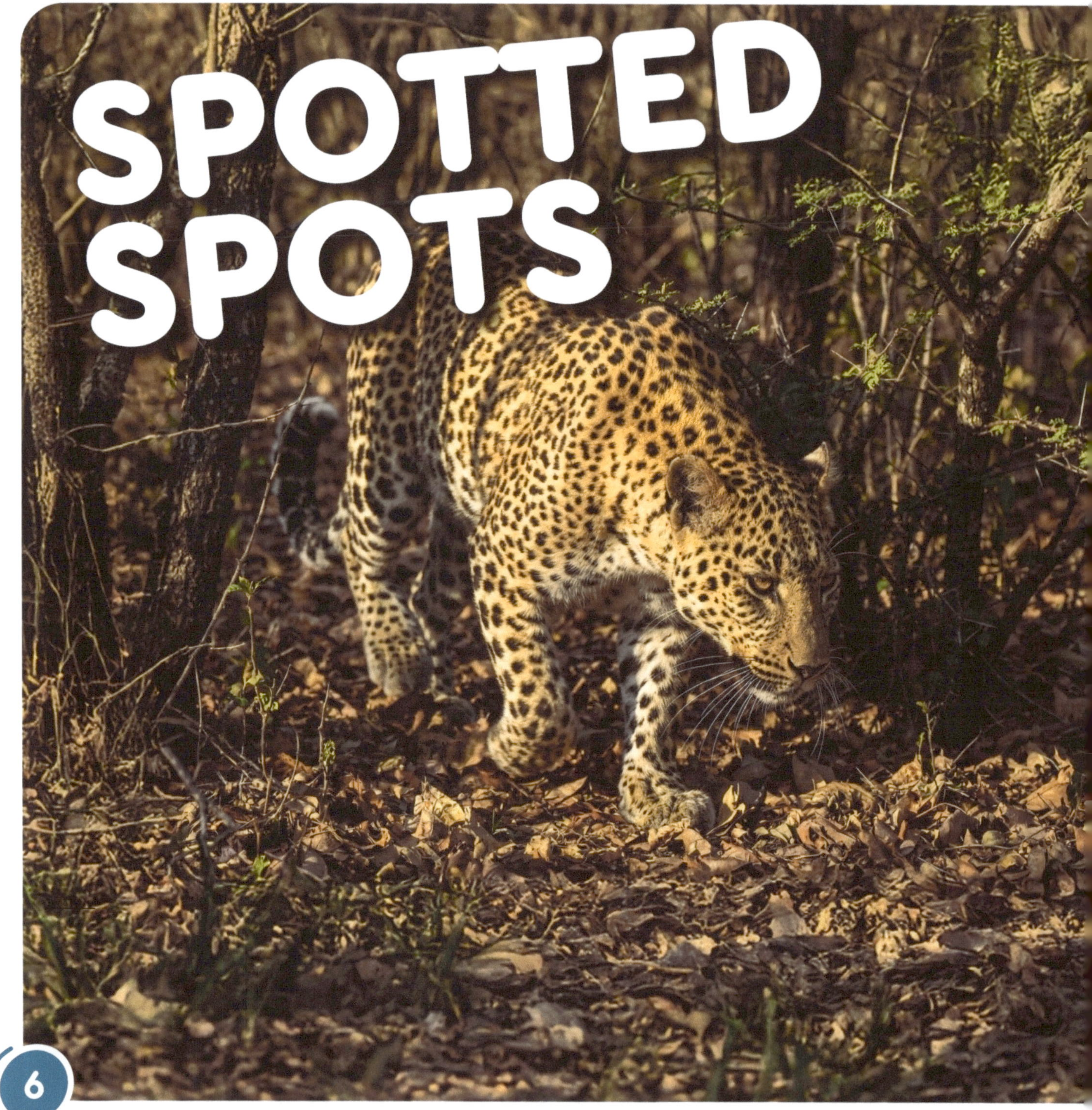

Rustle! A leopard moves slowly through dry leaves.

Leopards live in many places. African leopards roam in more than 35 countries.

Amur leopards live in Russia and China. Indian leopards live in India. Arabian leopards live in the Middle East.

Snow leopards live in the mountains of Asia. They can be found in countries like China, India, Nepal, Mongolia, and Pakistan.

No other wild cat lives in so many countries!

Snow leopards live so high up that scientists call them 'mountain ghosts.'

SIZE UP

Snarl! A African leopard stretches on a tree branch. It watches the jungle below.

Leopards are the smallest of the four roaring big cats. They are smaller than lions and tigers. But they are larger than cheetahs.

Male leopards are bigger than females. Males can weigh up to 165 pounds. Females usually weigh around 130 pounds.

These cats stand about 2 feet tall at the shoulder. Their bodies are 3 to 6 feet long.

Leopards can leap 20 feet forward in a single bound and jump 10 feet up.

A leopard's claws pull back into the paw. This keeps them sharp for climbing.

Snap! A leopard's powerful jaws close tight. This hunter catches prey.

Leopards have bodies made for hunting. Their muscles are so strong that they can carry heavy prey up into trees.

Leopard legs are short but powerful. This helps them climb and pounce quickly. Their large paws have sharp, curved claws.

A leopard's skull is wide and strong. Big jaw muscles give them a crushing bite. Their long whiskers also help them hunt by feeling in the dark.

Their spine is very flexible. This helps them twist and turn when they climb trees.

SUPER SENSES

Whoosh! A leopard turns its ears. It hears a mouse far away.

Leopards have amazing senses. Their eyesight is six times better than a human's. This helps them see in dim light.

Their hearing is excellent too. Leopards can hear sounds that humans cannot. This lets them detect prey moving in thick bushes.

A leopard's nose is powerful. It helps them smell animals from far away.

Leopard whiskers can feel tiny air movements in total darkness.

SNEAKY SPOTS

Thump! A leopard lands softly. Its spotted fur blends with the shadows.

Leopard spots help them hide. Their fur has dark rings called **rosettes**. These shapes look just like shadows on leaves.

Each leopard has a unique pattern, too. No two leopards look the same. Their rosettes are like fingerprints!

Spots help leopards stay hidden in grass and trees. Prey animals cannot see them easily. This makes leopards very sneaky hunters.

Black leopards still have spots! You can see them when the sun shines brightly.

MEATY MEALS

Hop! A leopard climbs a tree to eat it's meal it hid there earlier.

Leopards eat meat. They hunt many animals. Deer, antelope, and wild pigs are common prey.

Small animals are food too. Leopards catch birds, rabbits, and monkeys. They even eat fish and insects.

Leopards are not picky. They eat any animal they can catch. This helps them live in many places around the world.

A leopard can eat more than 10 pounds of meat in a day.

POUNCE POWER

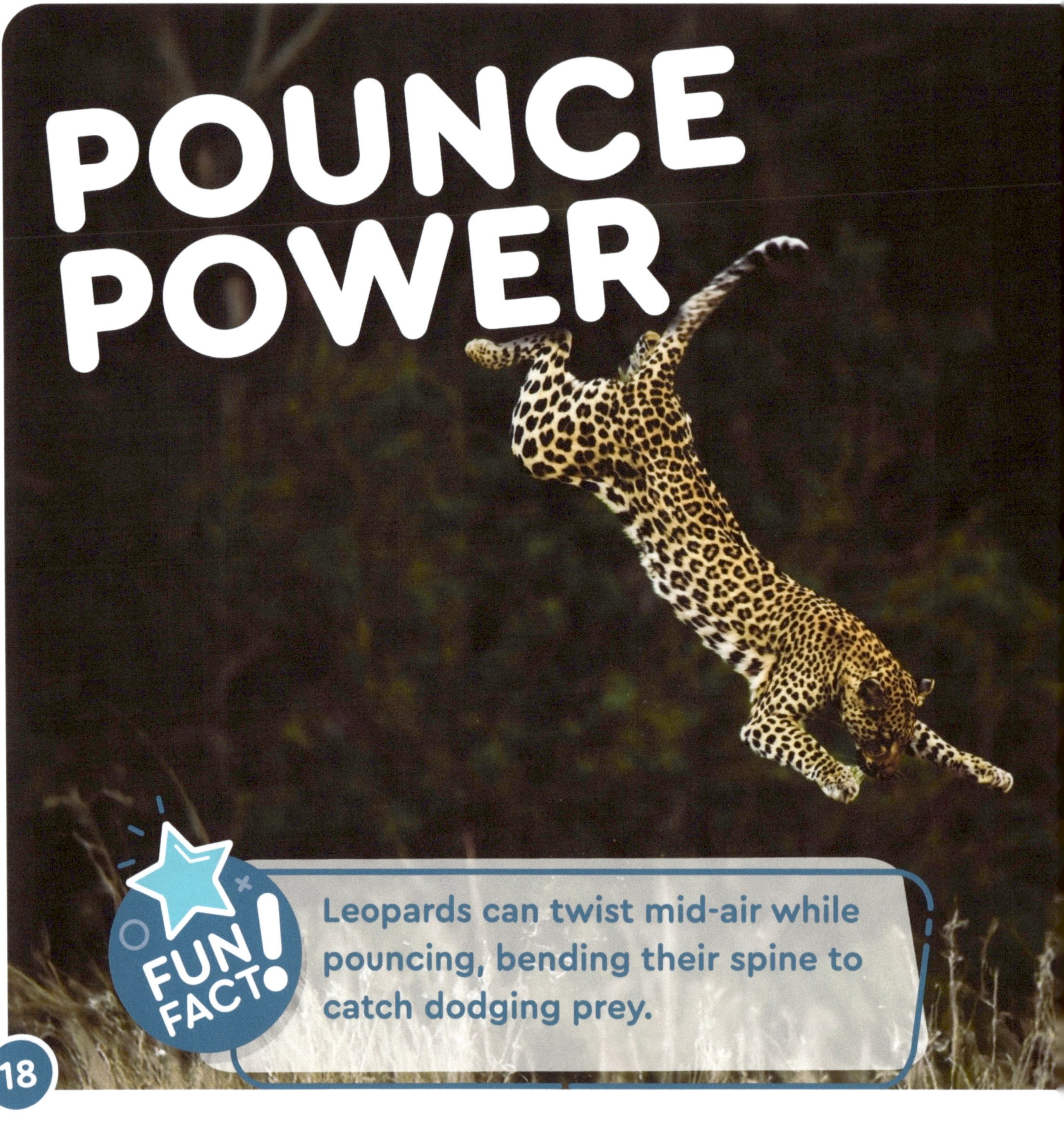

Leopards can twist mid-air while pouncing, bending their spine to catch dodging prey.

Pounce! A leopard leaps from a tree branch. It lands on its prey.

Leopards are **ambush** hunters. They hide and wait for animals to come close. Then they attack with a sudden burst of speed.

A leopard can run up to 36 miles per hour. But it only runs short distances, so sneaking close first saves energy.

When leopards pounce, they use their strong back legs to leap with great force. One leap can cover 20 feet forward.

After catching prey, leopards drag it up trees. This keeps their food safe from lions and hyenas. A leopard is so strong it can carry prey twice its own weight.

WATCH OUT
20

Hiss! A leopard shows its teeth. A hyena backs away.

Leopards face many dangers. Lions, hyenas, and wild dogs may try to steal their food. These animals can also hurt leopard cubs.

Leopards use warning signs. They hiss, growl, and show their sharp teeth. This tells other animals to stay back.

Climbing trees keeps leopards safe. Most enemies cannot climb as well. High branches are the safest place for a leopard to rest and eat.

Leopards can see in light six times dimmer than what humans need.

QUICK ESCAPE

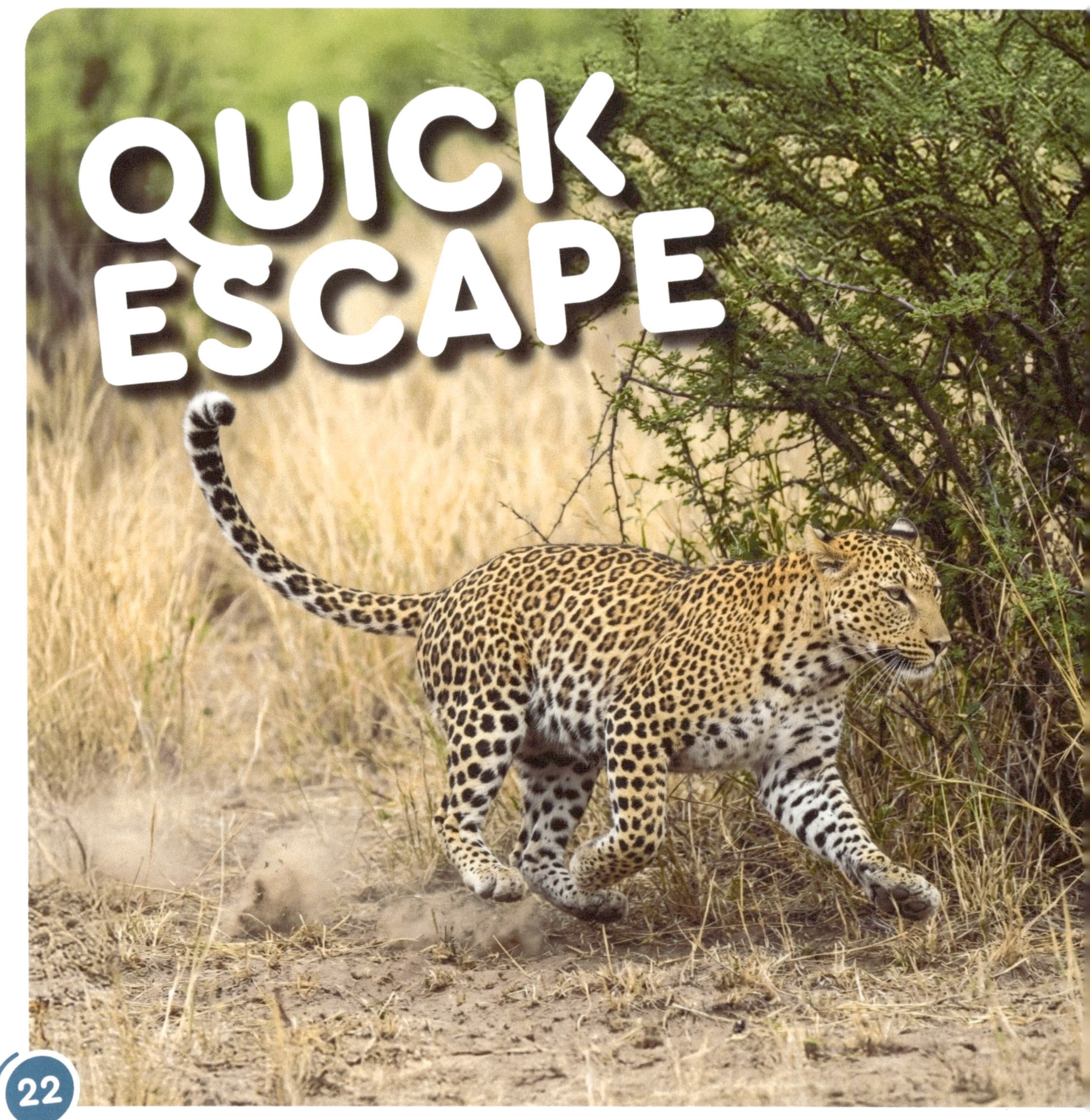

Swoosh! A leopard dashes away. It disappears into thick bushes.

Leopards run fast. They can get away from danger. Their strong legs help them run from threats.

Climbing helps them escape too. Leopards go up trees in seconds. Most **predators** cannot follow them there.

Leopards swim well too. They can cross rivers to get away. They move well in water.

Leopards can run at speeds up to 36 miles per hour— faster than the fastest human sprinter!

CLIMB HIGH

Screech! A leopard scrambles up a tall tree trunk.

Leopards are amazing climbers. Their sharp claws grip bark like hooks. Strong shoulder muscles pull them up fast.

Leopards climb headfirst going up. But coming down, they back down slowly. Their long tails help them balance.

They rest on high branches during hot days. Trees give shade and safety.

Leopards can hang from branches by their back legs while eating prey they carried up!

NIGHT PROWLER

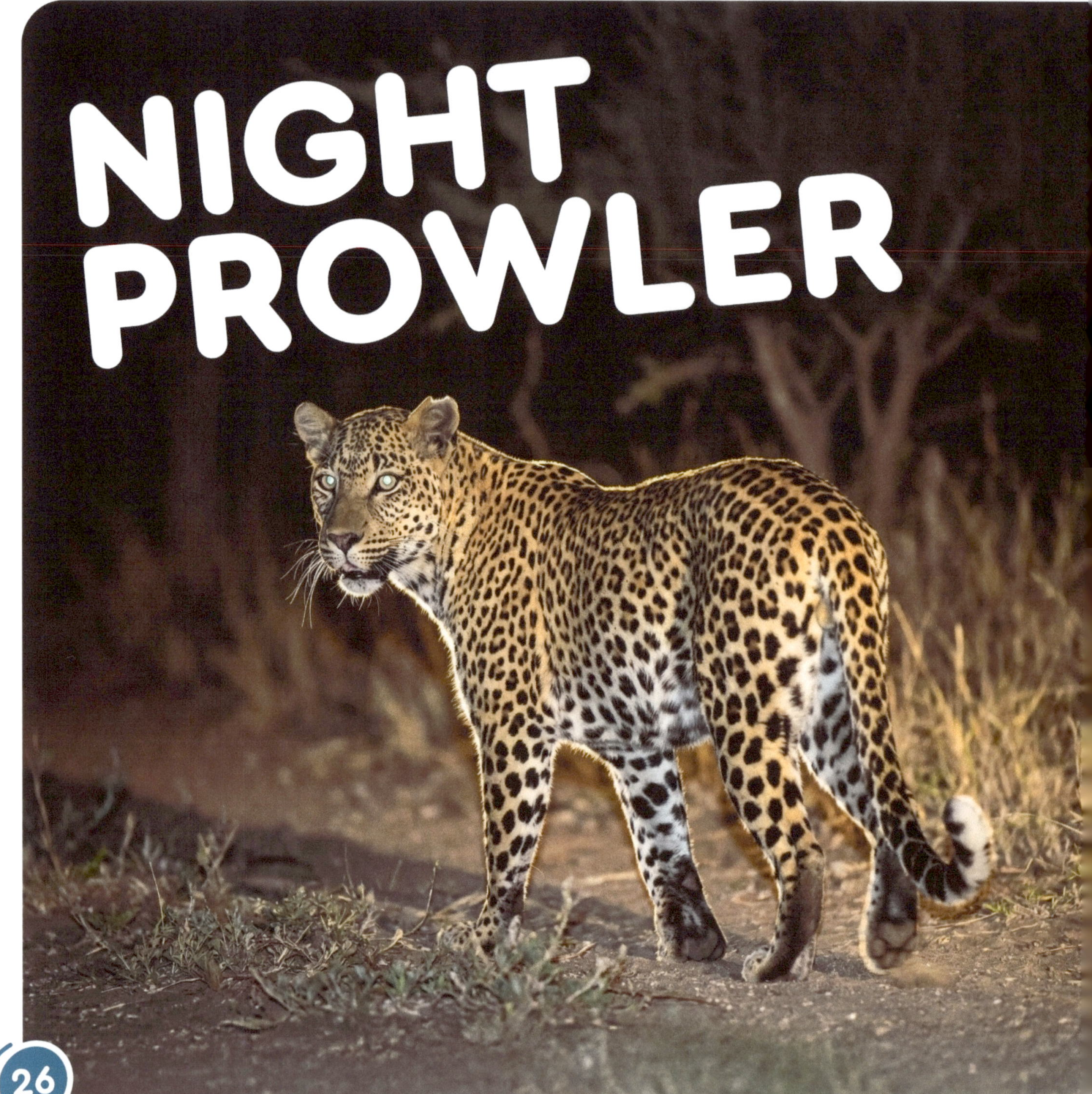

Click! A leopard's eyes glow in the dark. It walks silently at night.

Leopards are **nocturnal**. This means they are most active at night. The darkness helps them hunt without being seen.

Their eyes work well in low light. Special cells inside reflect light back, which makes their eyes glow.

Leopards rest during the day. They sleep in trees or thick bushes. When the sun sets, they wake up and start moving.

Leopards have padded paws that make almost no sound. They can sneak within six feet of prey!

LONE LEOPARDS

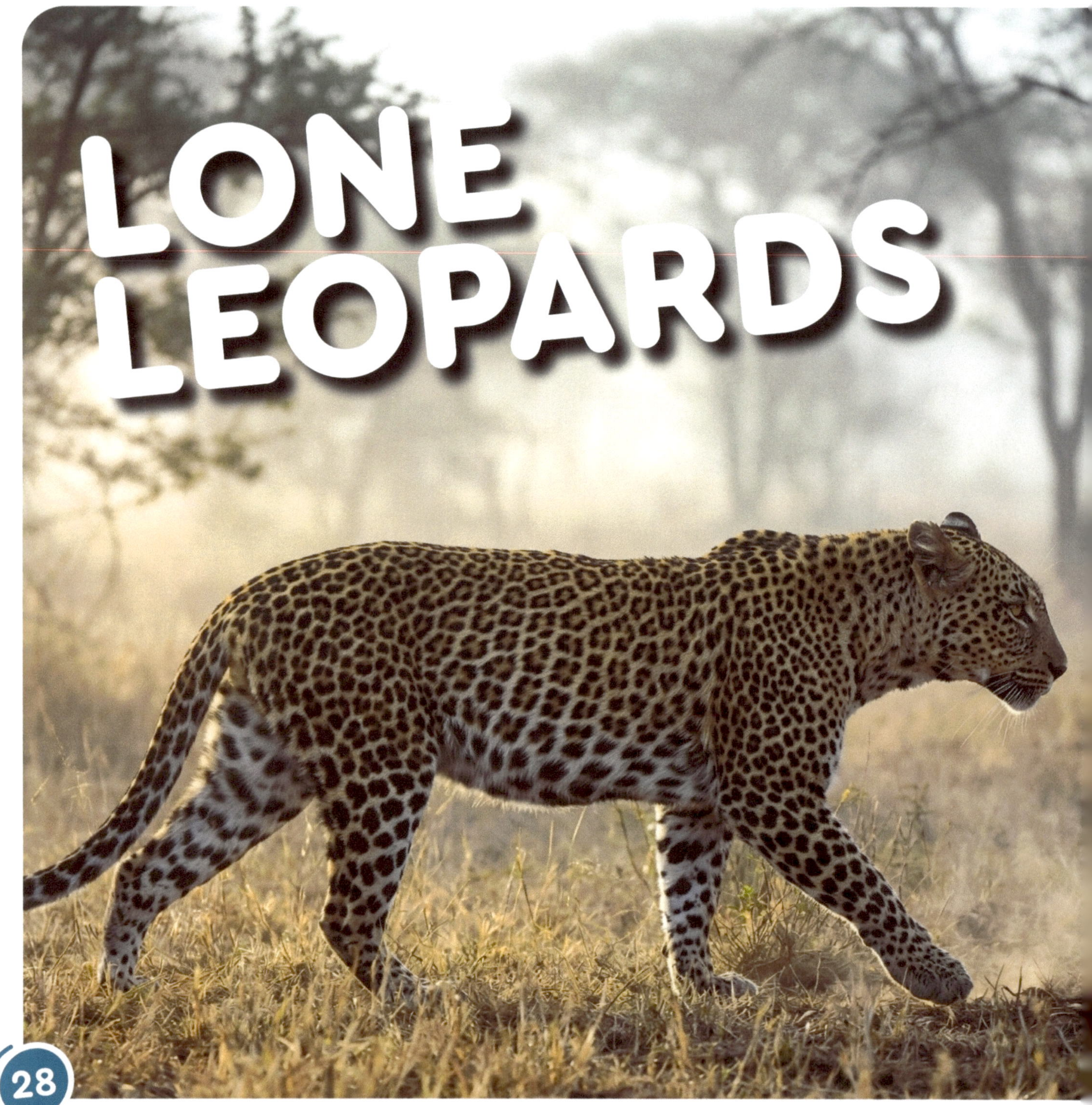

A leopard walks alone through the forest. It moves quietly.

Leopards live alone. They do not live in groups like lions.

Each leopard has its own land. It leaves scent marks. This tells other leopards to stay away.

Mothers live with their cubs. But cubs grow up. Then they leave. They go find their own land.

Male leopards have larger territories than females. Some cover 30 square miles.

LOVE CALLS

Roar! A leopard calls loudly in the night. It waits for an answer.

Leopards make loud calls to find each other. These calls sound like a rough cough or a saw cutting wood. The sounds travel far through the forest.

Male and female leopards live apart most of the time. They use calls and scent marks to find each other.

These love calls help them meet up to have cubs.

A leopard's call can be heard from up to two miles away. Each leopard has its own unique sound.

CUDDLY CUBS

DID YOU KNOW?
Leopard mothers move their cubs to new hiding spots every few days. This keeps them safe from predators.

Squeak! A tiny leopard cub opens its eyes for the first time.

Leopard cubs are born small and helpless. Their eyes stay closed for about ten days. The mother keeps them hidden in a safe den.

Cubs have fuzzy gray fur at first, and their spots are not very clear yet. As they grow, their coat turns golden with dark spots.

Cubs drink their mother's milk. After a few months, they start eating meat. They stay with their mother for about two years before going off to live alone.

MOM KNOWS BEST

Rumble! A mother leopard carries her cub gently in her mouth.

Mother leopards work hard to keep their cubs safe. They move their babies to new hiding spots often. This helps keep predators from finding them.

Mothers teach their cubs important skills. Cubs watch their mother hunt. They learn how to stalk and pounce by copying her.

A mother leopard brings food back to her cubs. As they get older, she lets them practice catching small animals. She stays nearby to help if needed.

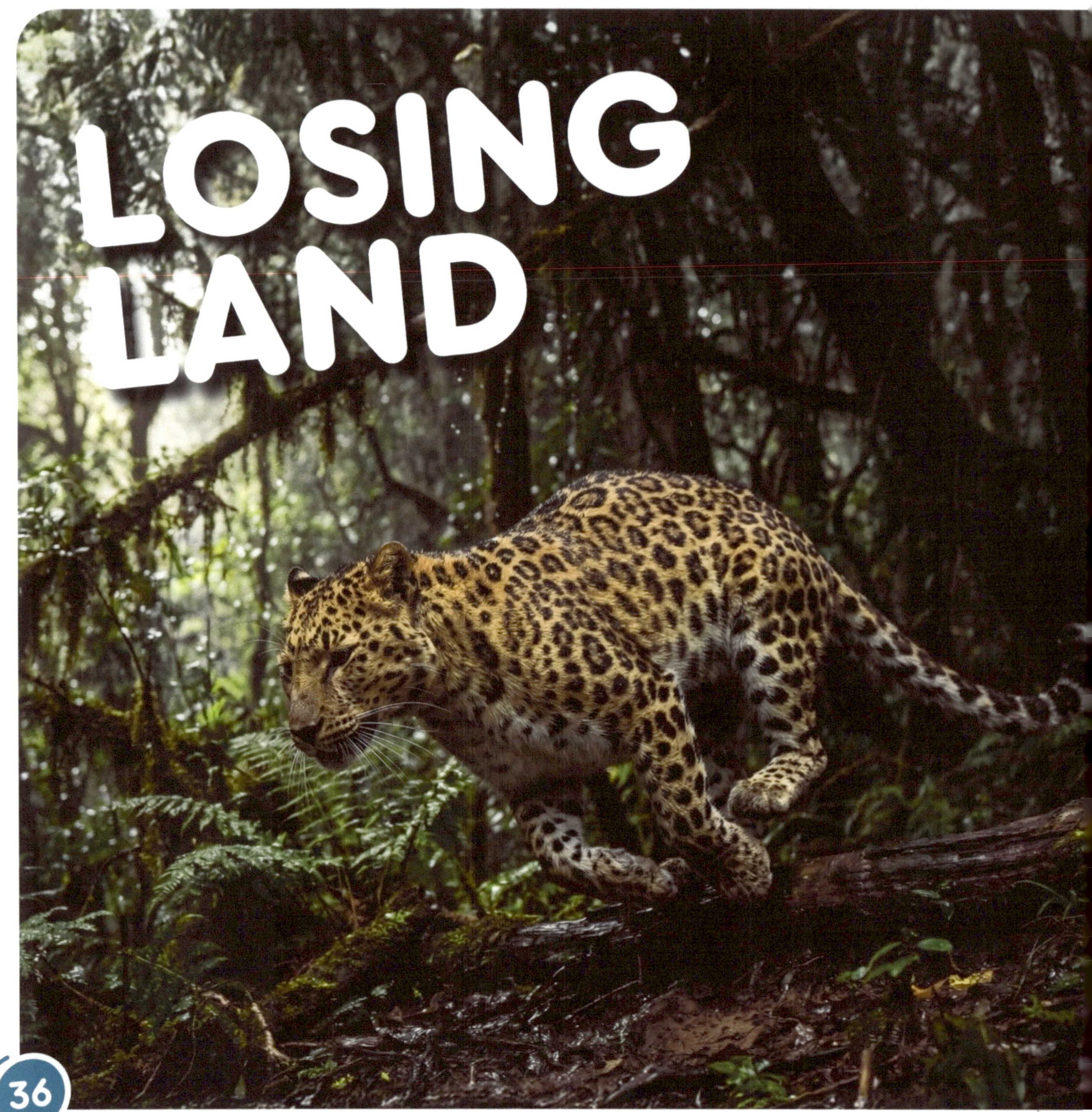

LOSING LAND

Crack! A tree falls in the forest. A leopard runs away from its home.

Leopards are losing their homes. People cut down forests. They build farms and cities. This leaves less space for leopards. They need room to live and hunt.

Roads now cross leopard land. Buildings go up where trees once stood.

When wild land shrinks, leopards cannot find food. They need large areas to survive.

Leopards once lived across most of Africa and Asia. Today they have lost about 75 percent of their original range.

SAVING SPOTS

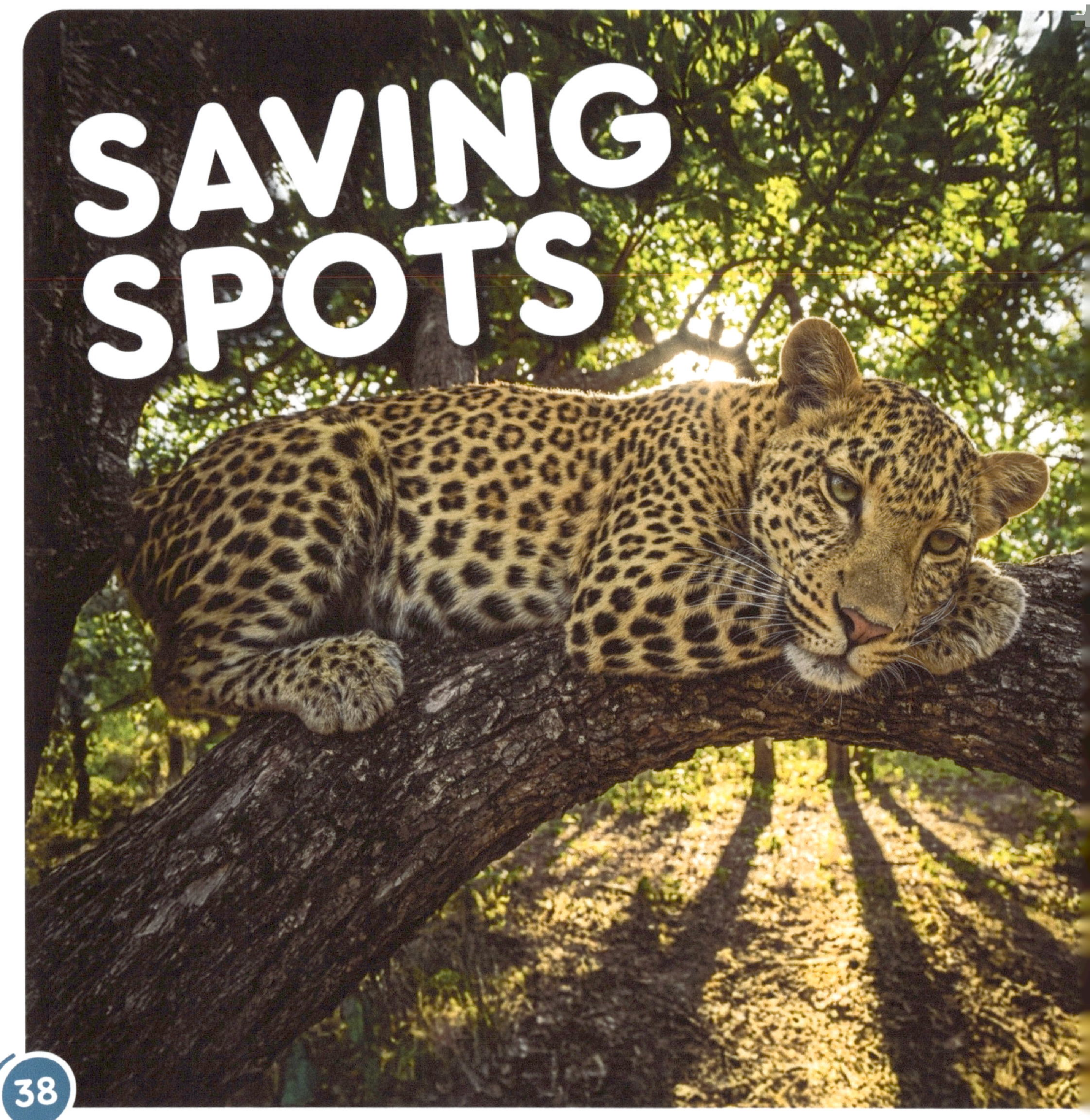

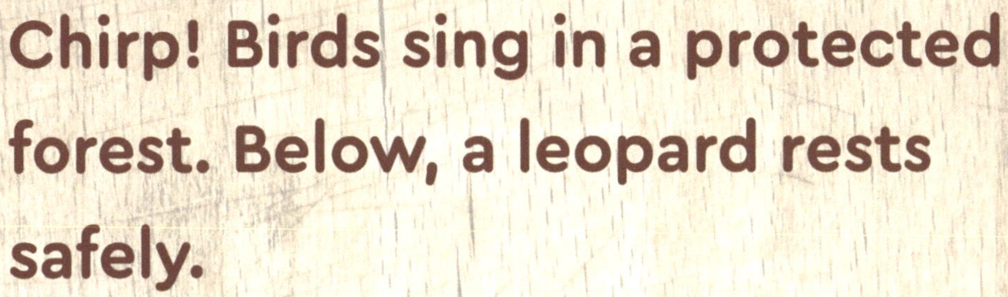

Chirp! Birds sing in a protected forest. Below, a leopard rests safely.

People work to save leopards. They use special cameras. The cameras help count leopards.

Some countries make parks. Leopards live safely there. Guards keep hunters away.

Groups help farmers too. They teach them to keep animals safe. This helps people and leopards share the land. Every effort gives leopards hope.

Some programs train dogs to sniff out leopard scat. This helps scientists study them safely.

GLOSSARY

ambush
When a hunter hides and waits to surprise its prey

habitats
Places where animals live and find food

nocturnal
An animal that sleeps during the day and is awake at night

predators
Animals that hunt and eat other animals.

rosettes
The black spots on a leopards fur that look like leaf shadows